C0-AZM-575

The Getting of Vellum

CATHERINE BYRON

salmonpoetry

OTHER WORKS BY CATHERINE BYRON

POETRY

Settlements (Taxus, 1985)

Samhain (Taxus/Aril, 1987)

Settlements & Samhain (Loxwood Stoneleigh, 1993)

The Three Shes (Verlag der Handzeichen, 1994)

PROSE

Out of Step: Pursuing Seamus Heaney to Purgatory
    (Loxwood Stoneleigh, 1992)

i.m. PEGGY DUANE GREENFIELD
1915 – 1999

Into the trench I poured
cold fluids for the dead
such as we living swallow –
honey and milk, sweet wine,
and finally spring water.
I scattered white barley grains
over the puddled earth
and began to talk to the dead –
the senseless, feeble dead.

I said: as soon as I'm back
home, back in my Ithaka,
I'll choose the finest heifer
in all the island herds
and slaughter her in my halls.
Here, so close to the River
Acheron, stream of grief,
it has to be this wild ram.
Even for you, Mother.

after
THE ODYSSEY XI.26-31

First published in Ireland in 2000 by
Salmon Publishing Ltd, Cliffs of Moher, Co. Clare, Ireland
http://www.salmonpoetry.com
email: info@salmonpoetry.com

Published simultaneously in England by
Blackwater Press, Leicester, England

Copyright © Catherine Byron 2000
The moral right of the author has been asserted.

A catalogue record for this book is available from the British Library.

The publishers gratefully acknowledge the financial assistance of
The Arts Council of Ireland and East Midland Arts

ISBN 1 903392 09 8 (This, Salmon Publishing, edition)
ISBN 0 952855 76 3 (Blackwater Press edition)

All rights reserved. No part of this publication may be reproduced or transmitted in
any form or by any means, electronic or mechanical, including photography,
recording, or any information storage or retrieval system, without permission in
writing from the publisher. The book is sold subject to the condition that it shall not,
by way of trade or otherwise, be lent, resold or otherwise circulated without the
publisher's prior consent in any form of binding or cover other than that in which it is
published and without a similar condition, including this condition, being imposed on
the subsequent purchaser.

Cover images and design by Denis Brown & David McGrail
Set in Bembo by Siobhán Hutson of Salmon Publishing
Printed by Offset Paperback Mfrs., PA

ACKNOWLEDGEMENTS

Acknowledgements are due to the editors of the following, in which some of these poems first appeared: *Anglo-Welsh Review*, *Autumn Journals* (Honest Ulsterman publications),*Critical Survey*, *Exposure* (Omagh), *Obsessed by Pipework*, *Other Poetry*, *Poetry Ireland Review*, *River City* (Memphis), *Soundings*, *Staple*, *Myself My Muse* (Syracuse University Press).

'Coffin. Crypt. Consumption.' was commissioned by the South Bank Literature Department for the *Ghosts* evening of new work, and was given its first performance at the Purcell Room, Royal Festival Hall, London, in December 1995.

'The Getting of Vellum' is adapted from the script of the same name commissioned in 1997 as part of the Arts Council of England's 'Write Out Loud' scheme to foster new writing for radio.

Artist-calligrapher Denis Brown has exhibited four collaborative pieces. *Couple*, on two calf vellums, contains the text of 'Examination of Conscience III' from 'Coffin. Crypt. Consumption.'; it was part of the 1995-97 touring exhibition *Words Revealed: an Irish English Anthology of New Lettering & Poetry* originated by the MAC (Birmingham) and the Crafts Council of Ireland. Three works on glass using the text of 'Amour Fou' were part of his one man show *Kalligrafen som terrorist / Exploding the Word* at Danmarks Grafiske Museum, Odense, Denmark, June - September 1998. Work in progress: *Birthday Suit* on vellum, using text from 'The Getting of Vellum'.

'Renderers' is the text of a Poetry Society 'Poetry Places' commission devised and published as a webpoem with the assistance and support of trAce – www.poetrysoc.com/places/cbyron.htm, http://trace.ac.uk/poets/byron/homepage.htm

The author is grateful to the Arts Council of England for a Writer's Award in 1997.

CONTENTS

I

Hotel Hades

WRITING ON SKIN

You urge me to use my blunt nail on your skin.
Just any word. I can't think, then start 'V' –
a downstroke. Lift. Another. The drag of skin
under my index finger. 'E – I – N'.

There's nothing there to see. Invisible ink.
Like when, a kid, I was into lemon juice
for spy stuff, words that dried unseeable
and needed a flame to turn them sepia.

...eleven, twelve... you're counting, and now 'VEIN'
is burning through like on a polaroid.
Thin rosy weals on the parchment of your wrist.
The word I've chosen, written in my hand.

AFTER PROPERTIUS I.xix

It's not the final darkness that I fear
nailed in my coffin, ready for the flame.
It's not death's cut-off point, the loss of name —
but that my passing won't be marked by you.

In that blind place I'd summon up our joy
greedy to touch you with my unreal hands.
Even alive I've been the ghost that finds
my love's obsession chills the air you breathe.

What if it's years before you follow me?
I'll haunt your future bones right to old age,
and down the decades how my embers' rage
will scorch you. That is how I'll live with death.

COFFIN. CRYPT. CONSUMPTION.

In 1397 the Aragonese knight Raymond de Perilhos made the pilgrimage to St Patrick's Purgatory on Station Island in Lough Derg. He wrote his will, and the Mass for the Dead was said over his still-living body, laid in an open coffin, before he was walled into the cave of Purgatory for ten days and nights.

i   COFFIN

I was cloudwatching.
On my back.
The sides of the coffin a tight
fit for my shoulders, the
foot end of it just
out of reach of my feet.
I saw the bruise of rain
moments before its first
spit on my face.
My tongue was out for
anything it could get.

Then the thrown pall
shuttered it all away –
wet, wind and heaven.
Blackness tight as a lid.
The absolute dark of
Blue John caverns
a hundred metres under.

It was at that moment I felt
like death for the first time.
Queried my state.
I swallowed and went within me
down channels and bloodways

– was it sickness or damage? –
potholing duct and vessel
tracking the dumb in me
that had never uttered before.

My searching tongue
offered lungs a voice,
but alveoli
half-inclined to mutter
turned over again and slept.
I was down where nerves
ran clean and autonomic
the innocent of touch.
I brought within me
skin's receptors
poised for adrenalin
rushes. Alerted
the buds upon my tongue.

All that interior smoothness
merely bridled, the tissue
rucking up and then
subsiding in silence..

The taste of me iron and salt.

Peccavi. I have sinned.
The blood of others is
sticky on my hands.
I have no stomach for it.

The first examination of conscience

There are bones
haunting the fridge
with mould on them like moss.
How many years now
since my carnivore days
when I picked the cage
of a chicken carcase clean?
Oh, and that pig's head
that I boiled for brawn
in a Scottish winter.
Remember how I needed
a brick to lid down the snout
when the boiling made the gristle
rear right up with the heat?
The brawn was clear and lovely
like a cache of garnet and pearls.
Never again, though. Never again.

The second examination of conscience

Eggs in a bucket
swimming in isinglass.
Whole eggs from the hens
the shells gone leathery as turtles',
whites gone all to water
yolk sacs slack and milky
so easily torn.
How I cashed in on their
mother-frenzy, my lovely
Rhode Island Red
Light Sussex cross
layers. From point of lay

to their moulting each Nov-
ember I forced them to be
egg-crazy, egg-a-day
wonders. I laid up
their overplus, stashed eggs
like oval ghosts in a pool
against their bald eclipse.
And all infertile: I'd
*coq-au-vin*ed long since
their solo cock of the coop.
Never again. I'll not
swallow any of that.
I have no stomach for it.

The third examination of conscience

When I bought the cleaver
at the butcher's suppliers
in the cold hinterland of East Kilbride
the man behind the counter
asked me quite straight
did I get on, like,
with my old man?
                              Fine.
Oh, I knew then fine
what cleaving was:
to split with a blow
or to hold on tight.
A man and a woman
shall be one flesh.
Cleave thou only
unto him. One flesh.

Come, Hades, lord of the inner channels
prince of peristalsis, potholer extraordinaire.
You alone know there is nothing at my core –
an extended nought, a hole from mouth to anus.

I have fasted for three days, and drunk no water
this last day – *light-headed, leaving home* –
I am pure pink for your pleasure. Thread me through.
This is the purest form of penetration.

This is the going up into the gaps.
This is the airy way of the hunger artist.
I beseech ye, o my bowels,
that I may not be mistaken.

ST PATRICK'S PURGATORY, JANUARY

Clear forestry of spruce and pointed frost.
    The road clangs like a bridge
across the timberwolf tipping of the hills
    to Lough Derg's edge.

It is the closed season, the pilgrims' boats are
    careened unseen, or any
way absent. Ice dip-candles stems
    at the brink, clouded, bony,

the slipway's bulbed with it. And the scarce sun blows
    the feathery gilt of light
onto stoup and stone, its circling station
    inched from northern night.

Construction site of McAleer and Teague:
    barges carry the stone,
the cranes, the dumptrucks, over. Purgatory's piled
    out over water, dun

and hard-edged, built with corridors and doors.

'THE NATURAL GATES AND
ALLEYS OF THE BODY'

Hamlet, Act 1.v. 67

The dearth of dreaming, when nights
were thin of wonder as the days
and the slow shutter guillotined number from number
of the month's exposures,
and transparencies came at last in a late post
stained with the orange of flare

I could not make either of us out

those nights when my world was instead
the World Service, and my waking eye
conjured on the bed's blank sheet
Russia – lights in the clouded snows
to the south of Moscow
India – the twisted ribbons of the flood plains
China – that red, red earth
and all those ears at their crystal sets
straining for the cut tones of English
that I used callously as a drug for sleep,
oh those willed and piloted waking dreams
dreams of the world's surface
through the double glass of pressure and altitude

and you breathed on unheard at our bed's rim

still unaware of the forced sleep that would end it:
canula poised in a vein – ear orifice angled –
to receive the spurt of slow oblivion
the op-art seconds when all complex seeing
slides into angular black and white
and simplifies and blackens and goes out

COCO DE MER

I was a blow-in, passing through, until
I overheard you talking about Horace
and his Sabine farm, as though it was
in this very townland, and Horace was your neighbour.
I joined you, we drank like fish – the dark stuff –
and you swore then that never again would you
cross the Shannon River, drive east to Dublin,
never re-enter the Pale of your finished life.
And wouldn't it thrill you to swear, and keep to it,
that you'd never even leave Gorumna Island,
not cross the first sea causey to Lettermore
nor the second to Anna-a-hyaan and then the third
to Ballydangan on the mainland of Connemara!

But soon enough, off we sped
in your red diesel Toyota
by way of Ballydangan
to the quay at Carraroe.
It was there, at the fish-houses
you'd buy us both what we needed:
our fill of aphrodisiac *fruits-de-mer*.

Back on Gorumna as the late slow dusk
burnished the lough below your slated cabin
we swallowed fifty sweet, garlicky clams
and a hill of crawfish prawns – pure protein.

Though we stayed in our clothes to talk about Aeneas
leaving Dido on the shores of Carthage,
and murderers you had defended in the courts,
and the purchase of yeast, in bulk, your contribution
to the townland's *poitín* still, a syndicate –

it was the moon undressed us out by the lough,
hurried us withindoors, and laid us down
on the chill and grass-bleached linen of your bed.
Skin to skin, how pale our nakedness
below our windburnt faces, in the moon's glassed eye.

And how lilac-pale your cock, a shy mollusc
I sucked into the salt swim of my mouth
willing it muscle, the engorging beat of blood.
Oh, mine was the tide that was inching back from slack,
and you out of kilter, stuck at some sad ebb
in your dead wife's grip. I could not tongue you free
but moved alone in the rising and return,
sensing by sonar, now, the pulse of the English lover
I'd left, not lost to death, though I'd put a sea
and half an ocean to wash
between us, wash him away.

How I loved you then when I'd stilled you into sleep
written goodbye and godbless in salt on your table
and gathered my cast skin softly
by feel and phosphorescence.

It was after moonset. Only the prickle of stars
silvered my road up and away from you.
I drove without lights in my almond-green Morris Traveller
and across the three sea causeys:
Gorumna to Lettermore to Anna-a-hyaan.
I switched the headlights on when I reached the mainland
and kept them on till I braked at Carraroe.
I turned the car's engine to silence, and stepped out
past the shellfish houses, and down the dark slipway.
I was dark, too, black as if in a wetsuit
when I slithered back into North Atlantic brine.

AMOUR FOU

It is
falling slowly
through glass

feeling each chill
mineral slide
slice in

keeping the cut
edges close

no blood

It is the last
gasp, the clamping
on ivory shucks
of air

It is
drawing the tackle tight
on the flung seine
of breathing

THE HOTEL HADES

In the old city, a shuttered afternoon.
The black redstart, lover of broken ground
warbles its song, a grinding of metal on metal,
a 'tsip tucc-tucc', and then its song again.
In the old hotel, shuttered siesta time.
Your cock rises again from its dark wood.
I take upon my tongue the dew of come
that's beading on your glans. My every mouth
is famine-hungry for you. I don't ask
if, where you've been, you sucked the cock of Hades.
Does semen count as seed? Like pomegranate's?

EGYPTIANS

i   *Mummy to tombrobber*

I have been stilled behind coursed ashlar
is it a hundred or three thousand years?
        Dry thorns score arcs on crusted sand outside.

The painter's rags are lying where they fell
when my flesh face was still a thing to paint.
        My bones are crumbling now like gingerbread.

The chink of chisel fiddles with my sleep
then you and light pour through a crack together.

Is it your eyes or light that moves my lips?
Is it your voice or air that wets my tongue?

By my articulate hand you lead me out
into the starlight like a lazarus.

You tell me that the room in which I lay
gave you a whiff of fresh delphinium.

        I would undo what you and I have done
        moving in starlight over shifting sands.
        I would retreat, and breathe again the air
        that's lost all savour but that errant blue.

ii   *Tombrobber to mummy*

Now when moon lies hammocked over trees
now is the time for penetrating bone.

        Disc over disc we make a strange ellipse.

My mouth on your pelvis, tongue hunts sacral beads
follows the milky way into your ribs.

Tightness of bone. Its dryness drives me on
to scatter arcs of droplets on your dust.

Starlight picks out their glisten, white on white

seedcorn of bloodflow and recurring tide:
here on the sandhills I put flesh on you.

iii   *Mummy's dream*

My cordage slackens.
Gilt indicates
my nipples' wasting site
slipped bitumen
through linen.
There is opacity
between my thighs,
my belly's packed
with resin, mud.

I dream your coming
dream my dilapidation
shored by you.
Your spacing eye
sees lintels where collapse
had shut down shape.
My frescoes startle.
Cleared conduits
run their fluent ropes
through rock.

The shaly marrow
of my bones makes blood,
its ooze is slops
and leakage. See
it spits on
dust's pale tension.

Come to me quickly
through the riven hill.
Cup my flow in hands
that crave this sweet
viaticum.

THAT WINTER, THAT SUMMER

i   November

Always in lamplight
or the cold's quick dusk
    we found each other

Always the tide of darkness
at our feet
or mash of leaves
    distillations of dampness
    that we warmed to

Always we nested
at winter's heart
    flaring the filament
    that found us.

Only one time
sun peeled back
gold-beaters' skin,
laid its lovely leaf
upon your face

        and I was Danaë
        visited by you
        slanting through curtains
        of my life's dark chink.

ii   December

There are secret exotic places
that fed me at my waking.
Will you be one of these?

Canyons of Arizona
emerging from mists of dawn
to a baked incandescence of pink

Treviso's poppied strip
as I walked into sudden summer
through the airless hatch of the plane

Will you be this to me,
a nectar record of heat?
I press my head in wax
working a flask to hold
this sweetness, this content.

iii   *February*

I am laying you down to landscape,
an illumination in my *très riches heures*
framing that night of deep prospecting.

Once you are land and sea and sky
the whole width of a lantern's looking,
I can hold you there in absence

walk up a damp track of you
survey the foldings of your green extent
from high passes through a pollen air.

But always framed, made from mere past
remembered. It will not be enough.

Can I conceive another passage through
thick glass of dusk, clanging the wicket gate,
stopping my ears and running home to you?

iv May

I enter the stubborn forest. It is May.
The ground is slimed with bluebell stems and leaves
of ramsons bruised to dark. I touch a tree.
The branch is dying. Bark lifts off like a sleeve.
Netting the sapwood are black bootlace lines,
mycelium that's spun invisibly
just under the rind, where juice once travelled.
Below, its fruiting body branches out:
honey fungus bright about the bole.

v   August

There is a knot of darkness in the hedge.
Black cock and hen are tugging moss and string
into its black. And here the intent cat
is watching, taut. There'll be no yellow gapes
out of that blank amongst the privet bones.

Within the whinstone sty there is a ledge
of death. A burst corolla of necks that strained.
Throats blackened with rot. A whole brood
starved above the hot breath of the sow.
Fork the dung – you'll find it red with worms.

Fry in the river spark like a welding torch.
Soft brome is lank with summer. There's a rush
and capsize into depths of green and heat.
Warm bodies burst like damsons where they fall,
release a whiff of gas that's sweet as may.

I MISSED YOUR RESURRECTION

left the golden city
by the wrong road

    passed clacking women
    weighted down with flowers
    in first spring's colours
    sulphur and bone-white

    pressed on to the palled
    hills of dead Judaea
    whence no help came

    smelt vinegar that one
    had scattered there

    burned asses' dung

Light grew behind me
clapped the pale flames out

    saw only shadows then
    on the shining road – my own

    never looked back

THE BLUE DARKNESS

I'm reading *Bavarian Gentians* and it's not death I see, or
   Persephone's shotgun marriage in the fields of Enna. No.

It's the long coarse throats of gentians gross as pitcher
   plants, lapped in the rangy grass of La Chartreuse.

Jos is wearing indigo jeans, Bavarian gentian jeans. His
   presence is marinading my innards to a soup. I lust
   luxuriously and on the quiet. He has no idea.

There are five of us on the valley road to La Chartreuse,
   down near the riverbed where the woodsorrel flowers
   are pale as shock, and forget-me-nots shake dull stars
   into the stream. Only the gentians hold the deep dye
   colourfast in their grassy spools.

A thin fire runs through my limbs. I am paler than woodland
   grass, paler than sorrel. I am seventeen.

II

The Getting of Vellum

THE GETTING OF VELLUM

Have you ever scribbled a telephone number, or a name
on the handy back of your hand?
Written something there on your own soft skin,
pressed and tickled across the grain of you
with the fine running point of a ballpoint pen?
It has the right ink that'll slide on
oily and easy, and stay there for hours.
Even a soapy scrub of your hand
won't shift it altogether.
It's perfect for jotting something down
in a hurry, something you need to hold onto
oh, for less than a day, maybe,
but vital for that day.
Paper is flighty, easy to lose,
and it isn't always to hand.
You'll not, after all, mislay
your own skin – will you?

Unlike the animal – lamb, or kid, or calf –
whose skin has been stripped off,
scraped clean of life's paraphernalia,
– flesh – fat – hair –
and transformed, even transfigured, into parchment
or – in the case of the calf – vellum
for the writing of the Word.

The monastery of Lindisfarne –
founded in the year of our Lord
six hundred and thirty five
on the island off the Northumbrian coast
known as Holy Island
that is cut off by the sea twice a day,
for several hours,
in the rhythm of the tides...

We've found so little
apart from cattlebone
and a certain amount of shell...

the bone is of early AngloSaxon,
early seventh or eighth century date...

and the calfbones are the most striking feature
of the bones that we've got...

So many calves, on this tiny isle's
scant pasture, and wild sand dunes
and reedy shores..?

The island is a small place, and no way
could the volume of calfskin be produced
on herds that were actually
born and bred on the island...

there might have been a specialised
centre on the island
where calves could have been brought,
and killed, and skinned,
so the calfskin could then be turned into vellum
for manuscript production...

A monastic abbatoir, then?
A vellum factory where the raw skins of
one hundred and twenty nine calves
were soaked and scraped and stretched,
their spine skin bound
into the spine
of the holy book they were made for:
the astonishing Lindisfarne Gospels?

Now the trimmed skin of their flanks
has been made into pale pages,
polished with pumice,
dusted with sandarac
against any trace of animal oiliness
that will halt the bite of ink.
And the pen?
A quill, a *penna*,
the flight feather of a goose
tempered and toughened
in a tray of heated sand,
then pared to a nib.
In the monastery *scriptorium*
Lindisfarne's Bishop Eadfrith
dips his goosewing quill
into vermilion ink
and inscribes the first words:
Incipit evangelium

That was thirteen centuries ago.
You can see the Gospels now, in the flesh,
in the British Library, under glass:
each illuminated folio undimmed,
the rawhide vellum white and stable still;
the calves' hides gathered
fleshside to fleshside,
hairside to hair,
but so transformed it's hard to say
which double page spread is which.

> *You know, the skins — I quite like,*
> *as a writing texture, just*
> *the little graininess*
> *of the roots of the follicles...*
>
> *Yeah, it makes like the*
> *surface when you haven't shaved...*

In the Vellum Works in Celbridge,
County Kildare,
in the last years of the twentieth century,
master calligrapher Denis Brown
is choosing skins from the fresh stock
of Joe Katz, Czech vellum maker extraordinaire.

Everyone has a different taste.
Some like them very white,
some people like to have
the yellowish old type finish,
then some of them, sometimes –
Denis takes the completely black one,
where there is pigmentation
still in them,
in other words, it was a calf
or a slunk
from a dark animal

A dark, yes... a dark animal
If you could sand that down...
This is one of the dark ones
I'd be interested in.

There's a body on them.
If I polish that –
that will become beautiful.

Beautiful vellum. Slunk vellum.
The most prized writing surface
for a calligrapher, even now.
This is the skin of a calf so young
it isn't even a veal calf,
hasn't drawn breath in this world:
a slunk, a slink,
a near-term foetus slung, or cast
by its mother – stillborn.

The getting of vellum starts these days
with the knacker's pick-up call at a farm,
the apparent waste of an aborted dairy calf.

The living calves
are already being weaned to the bucket.
The dairyman puts his fingers
into the warm milk
to teach them the hard lesson:
to suck from a metal bucket now,
not any longer from the warm flesh of a teat.
These liveborn calves
have been licked and glossed by their mothers
in the two days
before the dairyman parted them.

But miles away in the knacker's yard
there's no gloss on the coats
of the slunk calves
stacked on that mudded pallet.
Master knacker John Warman
lifts up the top one,
dirty black and white,
gangle of legs too long
for the scanty body.
He takes it, firmly, tenderly,
into the high workshed
and switches on the compressed air machine.

> *Born dead, a proper slink calf.*
> *Never breathed. You get a lot like that.*
> *Born dead —*

> *This calf — I probably picked this up*
> *Saturday afternoon. He still looks nice and fresh —*

> *When they come out dead*
> *they seem to keep better, y'know...*

The knacker's blade is long and narrow
like a silver letter-opener.
John Warman punctures a hole
in the calf's oxter
where one foreleg starts from its chest.
He pokes the airline's nozzle into the hole.

The hide of the calf's belly
ripples and balloons free,
untethering all the membranes
that anchor skin to flesh,
to gristle, to bone.

> *Now we don't touch that no more with the knife.*
> *I'll tell you what we do now.*
> *We get the skin down like that...*
>
> *anchor the hide to the floor...*
>
> *that's the hoist...*
>
> *See now, that skin*
> *by taking it off like that,*
> *see — there's not a blemish on it...*
>
> *Where you mark it out*
> *with the knife, just to start it off,*
> *you might just get a little bit of a*
> *mark with the knife, which you can't help,*
> *but the valuable part of the skin,*
> *all the butt and back and that...*
> *that's a perfect skin, alright?*

Who would have thought it needed
a winch and a steel hawser
to slowly, steadily, undress a calf?
Sure I can skin a rabbit

with my bare hands,
take its soft vest of fur
up and over its head –
rather too like
undressing a baby.
But skinning a calf,
a three days dead calf,
is another thing altogether.
It's like watching a birth,
not a flaying,
seeing the calf being born
a second time,
this headfirst slow emergence
from its skin
as if from the birth canal.
So dainty and delicate
in its glassy, gleaming pinks
and whites, its untried
muscles and tendons,
its organs – lungs, gut, heart –
never used ex utero.
Uterine vellum. Slunk.

> *A lot of people just want it totally clear*
> *and white, they're looking for*
> *something very consistent,*
> *more or less like a paper*
> *or a parchment,*
> *so you don't get the individuality,*
> *you don't get the markings,*
> *the faults, the holes...*

> *For me as an artist*
> *I'm interested in all those*
> *inconsistencies*
> *as a starting point*

for the composition –
like it may be even a hole,
I'll start winding a line of writing,
curl around it...

In the last years of the twentieth century
artist calligrapher Denis Brown
has set his *scriptorium* up
in an ordinary new house
in an ordinary new estate
on Dublin's southern edge.
In a might-be bedroom,
his workroom,
his steel pen has been
moving across fresh vellum,
a piece the shape and size,
say, of a gospel page,
but a dark pigmented skin –

A good calligrapher
will have his flow and his rhythm
and he will be able to sense the spacing –
it comes almost from your pulse, really.

He inscribes the word 'VICTIM'
and while the ink is drying
into the skin's soft nap –
he is piecing shards of glass
into a spiky corona
to halo that single word
from the Latin: *victima* –
living creature offered in sacrifice.

He fixes shard upon shard
to a frame of burnt wood
that will hold

skin – word – glass
together
in a charred box.
A razor-edged dark hole
that might hold:
victima –
vitella – little calf –
flayed skin shading a lamp

illumination.

BY THE CALF BAY AT LUMB BANK

It was the woman of the house
who reared the calves.
Did she keep them in this crypt
to have them handy?
Not as handy as the hens
but close enough.
And where were the cows
who'd dropped them only
a week, two weeks before –
before their calves were kept
apart, before the woman
trained them to the bucket,
her hand in the warm milk
making finger teats to wean them?
A cow is a fierce mother,
dangerous as a bull
in the hours and days after
she has dropped her calf,
muzzled it onto its knees,
and licked its coat
to whorl and peak
clean of the birth waters.
Were the calves' mothers taken
over the Colden Water
along Gamaliel Gate
to the high pastures –
or were they here, in earshot,
in House Meadow, that falls
to the alder and beech of the brink,
and the Water that runs always?

RENDERERS

In the Vale of the River Tas, South Norfolk

i   *from calf to vellum*

The milch cow slipped her calf
a slink, stillborn.
It gave her the slip
and sank through a fault in the earth —
a swallow-hole to Hades.

The knacker picked it up:
a casualty calf.
He winched off its skin
and laid the hide flat in hide-salt.
Its flesh boiled up for dogs.

The vellum-maker slipped the skin
into his vat.
He turned the paddles
and agitated the cream of slaked lime.
The hairs let slip their roots.

And now the nib of the letterer
bites the nap.
Scoured skin drinks ink
as if it were paper. Is inscribed
where once veins ran.

ii   from topiary to Taxol:
the great yew hedge at Rainthorpe Hall

Taxus, we render
Fierce medicine from your leaves.

Though evergreen
you make the patient shed
her hairs, unnumbered

and shed, with luck the cells
of refractory cancer
deep in her ovaries –

your own seed
a single ovum
in a fleshy cup.

iii   from junk to gesture:
the lapsed taxidermist at Gilt Cross

My work was once
all pets and roadkill –

how hard to stop the hair
and fur from slipping.
A day, two days at most –
too warm? All turns to jelly.

Now I want to sculpt
the structure under the skin,
the cogs and springs.
Anything but the skin.

Now my creatures are
all gesture, in junk.

She pencils in mapfolds
then paints the sections
in shades of old paper,
parchment, vellum.

She walks from the source
of the River Tas
at Forncett St Mary
her sketch of the river
like unravelled knitting.

'The paint,' she says
'is like a skin.
The earth has no skin –
it is flesh all the way to the top.'

Solvitur ambulando –
She has worked it out by walking.

'There is a mark only now,
where the footpath was ...
it has left a winding crease.'

ST THOMAS AQUINAS
IN MACNEICE'S HOUSE
September 23rd, 1957: South Belfast

This is our last autumn at Aquinas Hall, and today
Sister Dymphna is teaching us geography on a world scale
so as we can hold our own when we move to Secondary.
She squeaks a great chalk circle on the board
to explain the poise of this day, the twenty-third of September,
before the sun moves on towards *Capricorn*
and December's chilly *Solstice*. Today is the *Equinox*
when day is as long as night and the sun stands
right above the *Equator*, though you wouldn't know it
    in Malone
for a gale is battering down from the Black Mountain
onto the rain-blurred panes of the high sash windows
of our classroom, that used be the Cream Drawingroom
of the MacNeice family, before the Reverend was translated
to be Bishop in Carrickfergus. Would he ever have known
that Dominican nuns built their chapel in his rose garden,
their convent dwelling on the great back lawn?

Christ's kitchenette opens straight off the sacristy.
Sister Sacristan washes the dishes that have held
His Body, His Blood, here, in this ordinary sink!
And here, too, she scrubs and rinses the linen
that has been napkin under chalice and paten,
catcher of any stray crumbs and spills of Him,
drying cloth for the priest's fingers and lips,
wiper round of the chalice's fingerbowl:
corporal, purificator, words we girls only know
from the Catechism, the boys in our class
old hands at serving Mass. So Sister Thomas
takes us four at a time from Geography

for our Sacristy Lesson. All I can think of is crumbs
and smears and St Thomas Aquinas. Was he the one
who went on about all those angels on the head of a pin?

So what would he say about all the tiny bits
of Christ Our Lord being swilled down the drain in suds?
Each fragment His whole Body, like when the priest
snaps and snaps the Host when he's running short
at Communion, unto eighths, sixteenths, sixty-fourths,
and all of them Christ! Sister, Sister Sacristan,
what happens to all those Christs when you pull the plug?

Child dear, it is Holy Water, though not as Holy
as the Water I put in the stoups, or Water from Lourdes,
and it goes straight down into earth. Never fear it would enter
the unworthy, ordinary drains. See, I'll fill it and show you.

And we watch the water empty from Christ's own sink
with no spin to the left or the right, but in a perfect descent
just as, Sister Dymphna has told us, the water empties
from bath and sink when your ship *Crosses The Line*
and the sun's *Zenith* is exactly overhead,
and the contrary spins of the *South* and the *North*
Hemispheres are in balance, like *Night* and *Day*
today, at the *Autumn Equinox.*

                    And I know, without asking,
that Christ's Body and Blood descend in His Holy Water
to water the ghosts of the roses of Bishop MacNeice.

III

Blood Relations

MINDING YOU

You say you want to go home.
Shall I drive you there, one last time?
Across the water,
over the Bog of Allen
and the great Shannon divide –
home, to Ballinahistle?
To the field that has been in your head
from seventeen years old
to seventy seven,
the years you have been away?

This is the in-field, just over
the parkeen wall, and past
the ancient stand-alone thorn
and the line of damson trees.
Young Tony, your brother's son,
will show us again
the mounds and eskers of stones
he and his nephews have picked
like hard grey potatoes
from the field's ploughed lines.
Is it never done with,
the stone-picking in this field?

Seventy years ago,
your first grown-up work:
October potato-picking,
then the second
months-long harvest of stones
as winter's rains revealed them,
crop after crop.

I would take you now
and put cold stones in your hands
at the in-field's sodden edge,
lead you into December's
sticky furrows,
if touch, and step
could somehow bring you home,
here, in England,
to your own lost mind.

THE HUNT BY NIGHT IN THE BOOKSHOP

for Derek Mahon & Tom Paulin

I've glanced at headings
and no more than a phrase
or two on random pages.
New paper clumps so.

I will read on later
at a settled sitting.
How can I take such charge
here, without reeling
from fierce ghosts
ranting at my ear?
The smother of hills
tips its spilling curve,
the forgotten island is
bucking its anchor chain –
Rathlin, Mourne country,
names that tap my heart
to a reflex jerk.
The whole landscape
labours to butt through
the membrane memory.

Shall I shut the book,
post it back unbought
in its slim slot?

Once before, unwary,
I read on. Another
poet, talking of Ulster.
Halfway down a verse,
cuffed back by gunfire
from a shut-eyed boy,

a man slumps in his hallway.
His child is stilled
sole witness
where she stands
at an inner door.

I recognised
my uncle's doorstep death.
His daughter, eight years on,
still screams sleepless
in the Derry nights.

Rathlin and Mourne,
places I left her lifetime ago –
quick, to the cash and wrap.
I hunger to read of you.

SUFFER...

Lough Neagh, 1956
i.m. Mary MacNamara, S.C.M., 1945-1992

This is not sea, though the farther shores
are over the saucer edge of the seen –
islets of small scrub, rocks without weeds,
branches trailed with the pull of August leaves –
and the suck of it small, audible against
the green planks of embarking.
The eelman's boat is to ferry our whole crew
to the Bulls' summer island.
I choose the bench you've pitched to.

Low air and water are smeared
with the outboard's breath.
Last waders rise at its cough, and move
to different grazing.
We are caught in its sound
the clinker hull unreeling
unheard pictures of water. I see
the grease of caught eels coiling in the bilge,
heat rippling pink across the coral rust
of engine pipework. And then

the pipe of the exhaust
scorches your leg as you lean across
to sleeve your arm in the lake – Aah!
You will lie long nights after,
a cardboard box tenting the hot sheets
clear of the amber wound.
You will not cry.

Landfall jars us. Our rushes
and runs are tethered to a small acre.
You, with your bad leg, are lifted out
from the dandle of wood on water, sit
on dry earth, not minding, as we strip
and pass our skins under the scummy bloom.
Your burnt calf blossoms pointlessly with sap.

The grown-ups walk to unshutter the summer place.
Between their calls and our shrieking by the shore
you find a hobbled ass, finger its coarse
and cross-marked withers.
You tell me, as I dry, about thrown palms
the temple's golden dome, Jerusalem.

POSSESSION

There's a devil in my mammy,
    he made her fly
to the old ring fort
    on the farm that my
melodeon granfer
    wouldn't graze
with his heifers and sheep.
    In a celtic maze
she twisted off to France
    to a big chateau
and bought up the heirlooms
    of long ago:
a lizard vase,
    art nouveau tiles
bought in a Midlands
    junkshop, miles
from chateau or rath.
    The devil smiled
in my mammy's face.
    He was reconciled
to her nice capped teeth
    and charcoal hair.

Just her skin and her eyes showed me
    she wasn't there.

MY FATHER'S SON

Travelling east from Death Valley

I heard the voices of the women scolding:
– Other men's sons, he works with other men's sons –
Down in the Nissen hut he pulsed a stripped
frog's heart with rhythmic shocks. Its sinews flexed
and other men's sons stood round admiring him:
     – O herr professor –

I hear my mother's wail of proud reproach:
– Other men's sons, he teaches other men's sons –
Stonily staring at the Chevrolet's
soft furnishing, I refuse to be led out
to examine Utah's strata in the flesh.
     No no, professor.

     I am journeying east from possibilities
     from doing what other men's sons have done
     with another's father.
                    Alone I anatomize bikes
     spanner works into parts, power into idleness.
     Stranded in Utah, I watch as the gold men drink
     a whole month's pannings in a greasy glass.

I hear the voice of my father, weary now:
– Other men's sons, I have raised up other men's sons –
I will not mount that charger now or ever
nor travel westward, pricking through tumbleweed
to your laboratory filled with the art of blood,
     father professor.

MORBID ANATOMY

i

The ironing board cover, hot and steamed in use,
smells of liver cooking.

The very bowl of the empty iron spoon
tastes just like blood.

I want all animal fluids out of my kitchen
and translated to the laboratory
or the morgue.

ii

I want above all to be a first year medic
setting out at the start of the Michaelmas term
to meet my cadaver

who is waiting for me and three others
in the basement dissection room
of the Radcliffe Infirmary.

I want to tug at its drawer, feel the gliding momentum
as it comes out, fresh every morning
for our finest cuts

to spend eight weeks in that formalin-scented room
getting to know my quarter, getting right under the skin
of both of us

stiff and me, whether with scalpel blade
or my thinly rubbered fingernails. I'll be
unlacing felted

strands, teasing fibres and vessels apart,
concentrating on circuitry, articulation
of the limb I'm allotted.

I want it to be a leg, preferably the left, and to enter
the thigh's bundle of muscles slowly
through a layer of much fat

to work my way into the superficial and the deep
and then to the pearly sheaths that narrow
towards bone.

iii
As that first term draws towards a close
I'll want to go back to the body, at night
without my fellows

to be alone in communion with its wholeness
roughly reassembled

for only then will I want to ease the skin wholly
away from the flesh, make the integument into
a rumpled self-coloured rug

that the flayed body can lie upon, to become
an unclothed *Maja* or *Majo* in recline. I want to behold
my cadaver at three a.m.

and during the very last night of the Michaelmas term
I'll coat the peeled corpse in a three millimetre skin
of the clearest ice

and stand it up like the glass cadavers displayed
in a museum in Dresden:

a visible meat body, known to its core
with each of my five wits, save
taste alone.

No, there'll be no taking of it upon the tongue,
no chewing with teeth, no gulping it down
with saliva.

No cadaver tournedos. No human sushi.
And — greatest lack —

no knowing it deep in the peristaltic caress
of the hollow core of me.

iv
For the table I'd need roadkill, or a cardiac arrest:
a sudden felling, like that of the slaughterhouse
with stun-gun, or blade.

I know now that I need fresh meat, its oozings,
its slop and give: the pathologist's subject
or the carnivore's.

I am beyond the stiffness of the embalmed.
But I'm not averse to preserving fresh and soft
flesh myself, in my kitchen

pickling a thigh, say, to a sort of ham in a bucket
of brine and saltpetre

against the coming winter
and the new year's hungry gap:

long pig.

AFTER THE NUPTIAL MASS

i

I am closed to you.
I have been closed to myself
a sphincter tensed against all
introitus, my anatomy
rather like yours that I've
just glimpsed: no third opening,
all pleasure-points external.

That first wine we drank today
from the chalice, surely
that will loosen me?
Christ's blood will let you in?

Marriage is third-best
in life's vocations
but we have saved for it,
barring a once or twice
incontinent spill of your seed
unseen, contained below,
your face suddenly flushed
hot for Confession.

Tonight you press hard, harder
against what is this day
sanctioned for breaking, but
you cannot enter. Neither
blessing nor flesh, it seems,
will be enough to breach
my inconsiderate border.

So on our wedding night
I lie alone between our
brand new sheets while you,
a teetotaller, find
your own horizontal
elsewhere, in some pub.

ii

In the days that follow
I sketch your erections for hours,
standing male nudes in the
charcoal and deep red
of our first bed-sitting room.

How failure draws us close!
What friends we are! This
is our joy, we say, our victory
wrested in martyrdom.

iii

But after weeks on a list
I am brought at last to my real
marriage-bed: clinical,
under gas. The surgeon forces
a metal entry. Cuts and
constructs the woman I am
to be. How suitably I bleed
at this my defloration.

I wake wide-eyed to imprint
upon pain as my first lover.
For weeks it informs me of
each detail of my altered
inner geography,
that new-found bay of flame.

For months I cannot bear
to ease you to that interior.
And when at last you come
you are not any more
the explorer you might have been,
never venture far beyond
the mouth of the bay, never
make landfall in me.
Never disembark.

ALLOWING THE ANIMAL

After your father had come (I hadn't – didn't know
such a thing, not then) I lay on the blue-green
looped synthetic carpet pedalling air.
I even tried to hold a shoulderstand
to the count of nine, I was so keen
your egg should meet your sperm.
Would gravity help? Someone
had said so, thought that our problem might be
that your father's spunk ran out
too soon. Was I abnormally slopey?

I'd always been good at exams
and I only failed my driving test once
before passing. Why couldn't I get this right?
No one could say I wasn't serious,
stuck on this bathroom carpet between the bath and the door
checking my chart: yes, this was
the day of the temperature rise.
It was all thermometer and graphs
standing like puzzled fairies round your conception

like it was hospital ironmongery round your birth.
Suddenly now I wish that when you were born
I had taken your unshawled body into my unrobed arms
and licked you clean. I wish I had tasted
your vernix, our waters, our blood,
and then bitten the quieting cord in two.
Why don't we lick our babies?
Why didn't I lick you?

BOOKED IN

Is it the planned feel to it I fear –
the confirmed flight ticket with its carbons' slither?
The letter telling me simply 'You have a bed'?
Is it the vast spaces, the wrap in cloud
and the way gravity rules, and yet is lost?
Either way I know I'll be on my back
pressed into scant upholstery over iron
and someone else will be regulating my breath.
And either way there's only a small resurrection
after it's over, when the retro thrust
reins in the engine and slews the plane to face
the terminal building. Or the reining-in as pain
– the first step to healing, the surgeon says –
tugs me back from cloud to coming round.